T0064804

Jokes for Mom

Jokes
for
Mom

More Than **300** Eye-Rolling
Wisecracks and Snarky Jokes
about Husbands, Kids, the
Absolute Need for Wine, and More

— Jo King —

Racehorse Publishing

Racehorse Publishing books may be purchased in bulk at special discounts for sales promotion, corporate gifts, fund-raising, or educational purposes. Special editions can also be created to specifications. For details, contact the Special Sales Department, Skyhorse Publishing, 307 West 36th Street, 11th Floor, New York, NY 10018 or info@skyhorsepublishing.com.

Racehorse Publishing™ is a pending trademark of Skyhorse Publishing, Inc.®, a Delaware corporation.

Visit our website at www.skyhorsepublishing.com.

10 9 8 7 6 5 4 3 2 1

Library of Congress Cataloging-in-Publication Data is available on file.

Cover illustration credit: Getty Images/Vect0r0vich

Interior art credit: iStockphoto/Getty Images

ISBN: 978-1-63158-480-0
E-Book ISBN: 978-1-63158-481-7

Printed in the United States of America

INTRODUCTION

Being a mother is never easy—you work all day, whether at home or at the office, and you never get any thanks. Your family is crazy, your life crazier, and sometimes you wonder how you stay sane every day. Well, why not embrace the crazy? Why should dad get all the praise for being the "fun parent"? No more! It's time for moms to take their turn with embarrassing jokes, puns, and wise-cracks with *Jokes for Mom*!

Instead of getting angry or frustrated when your kids are whining or your husband is being his (lovable) annoying self, now you can whip out this book and leave them all stunned with your brilliant retorts. And why should dads be the only ones breaking out the groans? You'll find plenty of puns and one-liners in this collection that will have your kids mortified and face-palming with an outburst of *"MOM!"*

But why should your family get all the laughs? After all, these are jokes *for* Mom! Also inside this compendium of laughter are plenty of witticisms at the expense of your husband and children. Gather your girlfriends and sit down with a glass of wine (or a bottle—we won't judge) to crack up instead of complaining. Discuss the important subjects like evolution (why haven't mothers developed four hands yet?!), shopping (why don't they have Mother's Day sales? *Because mothers are priceless!*), and marriage (what's the difference between a new husband and a new dog? *A new dog only takes a few months to train!*).

No matter what level of humorist you are, this collection will soon have you throwing around sarcastic quips and embarrassing puns with the best of them! Let loose, have a little fun, and impress your friends and family with *Jokes for Mom*. Enjoy!

JOKES

1

DEFINITION: *MOTHER* (NOUN)—ONE PERSON WHO DOES THE WORK OF TWENTY. FOR FREE.

1

2

Cook a man a fish and you feed him for a day. But teach a man to fish and you get rid of him for the whole weekend.

3

Daughter: Mom, what's it like to have the greatest daughter in the world?

Mom: I don't know, dear. You'll have to ask your grandma.

4

THERE'S A LEGEND THAT IF YOU GO TAKE A SHOWER AND SCREAM "MOM!" THREE TIMES, A NICE LADY APPEARS WITH THE TOWEL YOU FORGOT!

5

A MOTHER SAID TO HER SON, "LOOK AT THAT KID OVER THERE; HE'S NOT MISBEHAVING."

The son replied, "Maybe he has good parents then!"

6

Why do mother kangaroos hate rainy days?

Because their kids have to play inside!

7

To Mom: I'm hungry, I'm tired, I'm cold, I'm hot, can I have . . . ? Where are you?

To Dad: Where's Mom?

8

Bought my mom a mug that says, "Happy Mother's Day from the World's Worst Son."

I forgot to mail it, but I think she knows.

9

A woman gets on a bus with her baby. The bus driver says, "That's the ugliest baby that I've ever seen. Ugh!"

The woman goes to the rear of the bus and sits down, fuming. She says to a man next to her, "The driver just insulted me!"

The man says, "You go right up there and tell him off—go ahead, I'll hold your monkey for you."

10

MOTHERS WITH TEENAGERS KNOW WHY ANIMALS EAT THEIR YOUNG.

11

Woman 1: I have the perfect son.

Woman 2: Does he smoke?

Woman 1: No, he doesn't.

Woman 2: Does he drink whiskey?

Woman 1: No, he doesn't.

Woman 2: Does he ever come home late?

Woman 1: No, he doesn't.

Woman 2: I guess you really do have the perfect son. How old is he?

Woman 1: He will be six months old next Wednesday.

12

A kid asks his dad,
"What's a man?"

The dad replies,
"A man is someone who is responsible and cares for his family."

The kid says,
"I hope one day I can be a man just like mom!"

13

Mother to son: I'm warning you. If you fall out of that tree and break both your legs, don't come running to me!

14

Two children ordered their mother to stay in bed one Mother's Day morning. As she lay there looking forward to breakfast in bed, the smell of bacon floated up from the kitchen. But after a good long wait she finally went downstairs to investigate. She found them both sitting at the table eating bacon and eggs. "As a surprise for Mother's Day," one explained, "we decided to cook our own breakfast."

Fred is 32 years old and he is still single. One day a friend asked, "Why aren't you married? Can't you find a woman who will be a good wife?"

Fred replied, "Actually, I've found many women I wanted to marry, but when I bring them home to meet my parents, my mother doesn't like them."

His friend thinks for a moment and says, "I've got the perfect solution. Just find a girl who's just like your mother."

A few months later they meet again, and his friend says, "Did you find the perfect girl? Did your mother like her?"

With a frown on his face, Fred answers, "Yes, I found the perfect girl. She was just like my mother. You were right, my mother liked her very much."

The friend said, "Then what's the problem?"

Fred replied, "My father doesn't like her."

16

A FAMILY WAS HAVING DINNER ON MOTHER'S DAY, BUT THE MOTHER WAS UNUSUALLY QUIET. FINALLY, HER HUSBAND ASKED WHAT WAS WRONG.

"NOTHING," SAID THE WOMAN.

NOT BELIEVING HER, HE ASKED AGAIN. "NO SERIOUSLY, WHAT'S WRONG?"

FINALLY, SHE SAID, "DO YOU REALLY WANT TO KNOW? WELL, I'LL TELL YOU. I HAVE COOKED AND CLEANED AND FED THE KIDS FOR 15 YEARS AND ON MOTHER'S DAY, YOU DON'T EVEN TELL ME SO MUCH AS 'THANK YOU.'"

"WHY SHOULD I?" HE SAID. "NOT ONCE IN 15 YEARS HAVE I HAD A FATHER'S DAY GIFT."

"YES," SHE SAID, "BUT I'M THEIR REAL MOTHER."

17

A little girl asked her mom, "How did the human race appear?"

Her mom answered, "God made Adam and Eve and they had children, and so all mankind was made. . . ."

Two days later, the girl asked her dad the same question. Her dad answered, "Many years ago there were monkeys from which the human race evolved."

The confused girl returned to her mom and said, "Mom, how is it possible that you told me the human race was created by God, and Dad said they developed from monkeys?"

The mother answered, "Well, dear, it is very simple. I told you about my side of the family and your father told you about his!"

WHY IS MOTHER'S DAY BEFORE FATHER'S DAY?

So that the kids can spend all their Christmas money on Mom.

Two men are talking, and one says to the other, "My wife's doctor says she has menopause, and, man, has she been moody lately. How long do the symptoms of menopause usually last?"

The other man replies, "Let me put it this way: menopause will be listed as the cause on your death certificate."

Son: When is Mother's Day, Dad?

Dad, wearily unplugging the vacuum:
"Every day, son, every day."

A mother is trying to get her son to eat carrots. "Carrots are good for your eyes," she says.

"How do you know?" the son asks.

The mother replies, "Have you ever seen a rabbit wearing glasses?"

22

DEFINITION:
SWEATER (NOUN)—
SOMETHING YOU
WEAR WHEN YOUR
MOTHER GETS COLD.

23

Mom: Someone with the amazing ability to hear a sneeze through three closed doors in the middle of the night, three bedrooms away . . . while Dad snores next to her.

If evolution really works, how come mothers only have two hands?

A kid walks up to his mom and asks, "Mom, can I go bungee jumping?"

The mom says "No, you were born from broken rubber and I don't want you to go out the same way!"

26

Son: Mom, why are computers so smart?

Mom: They listen to their motherboard.

27

IT IS NEVER EASY BEING A MOTHER. IF IT WERE EASY, FATHERS WOULD DO IT.

28

You will always be your child's favorite toy.

29

WHY IS DAENERYS TARGARYEN THE PATRON SAINT OF MOTHER'S DAY?

Because she's the mother of all dragons.

30

If your kids are giving you a headache, follow the directions on the aspirin bottle, especially the part that says "keep away from children."

31

Son: "Mom, stop making jokes, they're not funny."

Mom: "I made you, didn't I?"

32

People who say they sleep like a baby don't have one.

33

SON TO MOTHER: "HAPPY MOTHER'S DAY. SORRY I WRECKED YOUR VAGINA."

Daughter: Mom, I need my personal space!

Mom: You came out of my personal space.

Son: Mom, Dad keeps making Dad jokes!

Mom: So?

Son: So, what's a Mom joke?

Mom: Look in the mirror, dear.

36

I SAW MOMMY ASKING SANTA WHY HE DIDN'T PUT HIS DISHES IN THE DISHWASHER.

37

Sunday school teacher: Tell me, Johnny. Do you say prayers before eating?

Johnny: No, ma'am, I don't have to. My mom's a good cook.

38

A boy goes to a strip club.

Mom: Did you see anything there that you were not supposed to see?

Boy: Yes, I saw Dad!

39

Why don't they have Mother's Day sales?

Because mothers are priceless.

What's the difference between Superman and mothers?

Superman's just a superhero now and then. Mothers are superheroes all the time.

What three words solve Dad's every problem?

"Ask your mother."

42

WHAT'S THE HARDEST THING YOUR MOTHER MAKES YOU SWALLOW?

The fact they're always right.

43

Knock, knock

Who's there?

Annie

Annie who?

Annie thing you can do, Mom can do better.

44

Knock, Knock.
Who's there?
Water.
Water who?
Water you doing for Mother's Day?

45

Knock, knock!
Who's there?
Justin!
Justin who?
Justin time for Mother's Day!

46

I SHOUTED TO MY MOM ON MOTHER'S DAY, "HOW DOES BREAKFAST IN BED SOUND?" SHE SAID, "OOH, THAT SOUNDS LOVELY! I SAID, "GREAT, I'LL HAVE BACON, HASHBROWNS, AND TWO EGGS."

47

I asked Mom what she wanted for Mother's Day. She said, "A bit of care and comfort." So I put her in a nursing home.

48

**I really wanted a game console, so I presented
my mom with a PlayStation 4 for Mother's Day.
She said, "Why am I not surprised?"
I replied, "Because there's no wrapping paper?"**

49

"One day's vacation a year, that's all I get!" complains
the woman.
Her boss replies, "Well, we call it Mother's Day and
technically you still have to work."

50

I BET MOTHER'S DAY GETS REALLY AWKWARD AND CONFUSING ON *GAME OF THRONES*.

51

Why do Mothers have to have two visits to the optometrist?

Because they also have eyes in the back of their head.

52

For weeks, six-year-old Tommy kept telling his first-grade teacher about the baby brother or sister that was expected at his house.

One day, the mother allowed the boy to feel the movements of the unborn child. The six-year old was obviously impressed but made no comment. Afterward, he stopped telling his teacher about the impending event.

The teacher finally sat the boy down and said, "Tommy, whatever has become of that baby brother or sister you were expecting at home?"

Tommy burst into tears and confessed, "I think Mommy ate it!"

ONE DAY, A LITTLE GIRL WAS SITTING AND WATCHING HER MOTHER DO THE DISHES AT THE KITCHEN SINK. SHE SUDDENLY NOTICED THAT HER MOTHER HAD SEVERAL STRANDS OF WHITE HAIR STANDING OUT IN CONTRAST TO HER BRUNETTE HAIR. SHE LOOKS AT HER MOTHER AND ASKS, "WHY ARE SOME OF YOUR HAIRS WHITE, MOM?"

HER MOTHER REPLIED, "WELL, EVERY TIME THAT YOU DO SOMETHING WRONG AND MAKE ME CRY OR UNHAPPY, ONE OF MY HAIRS TURNS WHITE."

THE LITTLE GIRL THOUGHT ABOUT THIS REVELATION FOR A WHILE AND THEN ASKED, "MOMMA, HOW COME ALL OF GRANDMA'S HAIRS ARE WHITE?"

54

A MOTHER'S SACRIFICE ISN'T GIVING BIRTH. IT'S NINE MONTHS WITHOUT WINE.

55

Daughter to Mom: Happy Mother's Day to someone who spoils me and then complains about how spoiled I am.

56

Woman 1: Why are you drinking wine out of a coffee mug?

Woman 2: I have to; it was getting embarrassing. Every time my daughter saw a wine glass she would point and cry out, "Mommy, Mommy!"

57

The family was disappointed with their Mother's Day celebrations on the moon.

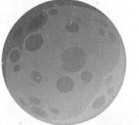

The food was terrific, but the restaurant lacked atmosphere.

58

Children: You spend the first 2 years of their life teaching them to walk and talk. Then you spend the next 16 years telling them to sit down and shut up.

59

WHENEVER I FILL OUT AN APPLICATION, IN THE PART THAT SAYS "IN CASE OF EMERGENCY, NOTIFY:" I PUT "DOCTOR." WHAT'S MY MOTHER GOING TO DO?

60

Mother: Why is there a strange baby in the crib?
Daughter: You told me to change the baby.

61

1st baby: You begin wearing maternity clothes as soon as your OB/GYN confirms your pregnancy.
2nd baby: You wear your regular clothes for as long as possible.
3rd baby: Your maternity clothes ARE your regular clothes.

62

How do your kids know that you're cross with them?

You use their full name.

63

A mother mouse and a baby mouse are walking along when suddenly a cat attacks them. The mother mouse shouts "BARK!" and the cat runs away.

"See?" the mother mouse says to her baby. "Now do you see why it's important to learn a foreign language?"

64

9 THINGS MOM WOULD NEVER SAY

1. "How on earth can you see the TV sitting so far back?"

2. "Yeah, I used to skip school a lot, too."

3. "Just leave all the lights on . . . it makes the house look cheerier."

4. "Let me smell that shirt—yeah, it's good for another week."

5. "Go ahead and keep that stray dog, honey. I'll be glad to feed and walk him every day."

6. "Well, if Rahul's mamma says it's okay, that's good enough for me."

7. "The curfew is just a general time to shoot for. It's not like I'm running a prison around here."

8. "I don't have a tissue with me . . . just use your sleeve."

9. "Don't bother wearing a jacket—the wind chill is bound to improve."

65

Little girl to her friend: "I'm never having kids. I hear they take nine months to download."

66

There's a debate about when a fetus is considered a real person. For Jewish mothers, it's not until the child enters medical school.

67

What did the mother rope say to her child?

"Don't be knotty."

68

WHAT DID THE DIGITAL CLOCK SAY TO ITS MOTHER?

"Look, Ma! No hands!"

69

"Mom, are bugs good to eat?" asked the boy.

"Let's not talk about such things at the dinner table, son," his mother replied. After dinner the mother inquired, "Now, baby, what did you want to ask me?"

"Oh, nothing," the boy said. "There was a bug in your soup, but now it's gone."

70

Boy: Hey mom, can I have a hundred dollars?

Mom: Son, money doesn't grow on trees.

Boy: Where does money come from?

Mom: Paper.

Boy: Where does paper come from?

Mom: . . .

71

WHAT DID MOMMY SPIDER SAY TO BABY SPIDER?

You spend too much time on the web.

72

Why do Jewish mothers make great parole officers?

They never let anyone finish a sentence!

73

WHAT DID THE MOTHER
BROOM SAY TO THE BABY
BROOM**?**

It's time to go to sweep!

74

**A police recruit was asked during the exam,
"What would you do if you had to arrest your
own mother?"**

He said, "Call for backup."

75

Mother to daughter: "What kind of person is your new boyfriend? Is he respectable?"

"Of course he is, Mom. He's thrifty, doesn't drink or smoke, and has a very nice wife and three well-behaved children."

76

A child comes home from his first day at school. His mother asks, "What did you learn today?"
The kid replies, "Not enough. I have to go back tomorrow."

77

WHY DO BEES HUM?

Because they don't know
the words.

78

What kind of bird can write?

A pen-guin

79

What did the buffalo say to her son before he left?

Bison.

80

What do you call a fly with no wings?

A walk.

81

Why did the dinosaur cross the road?

Because the chicken hadn't been invented yet.

82

Why did the boy bring toilet paper to the party?

Because he was a party pooper.

83

WHY IS EVERYONE TIRED ON APRIL FIRST?

Because they've just finished a 31-day March.

84

What's brown and sounds like a bell?

Dung.

85

What's the difference between a dirty bus stop and a lobster with breast implants?

One is a crusty bus station and the other is a busty crustacean.

86

WHY ARE FISH SO SMART?

They live in schools.

87

How do you know that it's raining cats and dogs?

You step in a poodle.

88

What do you call a sheep with no head or legs?

A cloud.

89

WHAT DO YOU CALL CHEESE THAT'S NOT YOURS?

Nacho cheese.

90

How do you make a tissue dance?

Put a little boogie in it.

91

How do you wake up Lady Gaga?

P-P-P-Poke her face, P-P-P-Poke her face!

92

Why did Tigger look in the toilet?

Because he was looking for Pooh!

93

WHERE DO YOU FIND A DOG WITH NO LEGS?

The same place you left him.

94

What do you call a dog with a surround sound system?

A sub-woofer.

95

When do you go at red and stop at green?

When you're eating a watermelon!

96

What's a dinosaur's favorite reindeer?

Comet.

97

What kind of bird steals?

A robin.

98

What does a vampire snowman give you?

Frostbite!

54

99

WHERE ARE THE BEST PENCILS MADE?

Pencil-vania.

100

What time do you go to the dentist?

At 2:30 (tooth-hurty)!

101

WHAT GETS WETTER THE MORE IT DRIES?

A towel!

102

Knock Knock.
Who's there?
Kent.
Kent who?
Kent you let me in?

103

Knock Knock.

Who's there?

Ears.

Ears who?

Ears some more knock knock jokes for you.

104

Knock Knock.

Who's there?

Woo.

Woo who?

You don't need to cheer. It's just a joke.

105

KNOCK KNOCK.
Who's there?
TANK.
Tank who?
YOU ARE WELCOME.

106

Knock Knock.
Who's there?
Adore.
Adore who?
Adore is between us. Open up!

107

Knock Knock.

Who's there?

Ya.

Ya who?

Wow. You sure are excited to see me!

108

Knock Knock.

Who's there?

Cows go.

Cows go who?

Cows don't go who, they go moo.

109

Knock Knock.
Who's there?
Etch.
Etch who?
Bless you!

110

Knock Knock.
Who's there?
I am.
I am who?
Oh no! Did you forget your name?

111

KNOCK KNOCK.
Who's there?
A LITTLE OLD LADY.
A little old lady who?
I DIDN'T KNOW YOU COULD YODEL.

112

Knock Knock.
Who's there?
Spell.
Spell who?
W-H-O.

113

Knock Knock.

Who's there?

Smell mop.

Smell mop who?

Smell mop who?! (say it really loudly)

114

Knock knock

Who's there?

Beats!

Beats who?

Beats me!

115

Knock, knock
Who's there?
Ada.
Ada who?
Ada burger for lunch!

116

KNOCK! KNOCK!
Who's there?
CLAIRE.
Claire who?
CLAIRE THE WAY; I'M COMING IN!

117

Knock knock
Who's there?
Frank!
Frank who?
Frank you for being my friend!

Knock, knock
Who's there?
Alpaca.
Alpaca who?
Alpaca the trunk, you pack the suitcase!

119

Knock, knock
Who's there?
Who.
Who who?
Is there an owl in here?

120

I'VE TRAINED MY DOG TO BRING ME A GLASS OF RED WINE.

It's a Bordeaux collie.

121

I'M A WINE ENTHUSIAST.

The more wine I drink, the more enthusiastic I get.

122

What did the grape say when it was crushed?

Nothing, it just let out a little wine.

123

I was sat with my wife while she sipped on her glass of wine, when she said, "I love you so much, you know. I don't know how I could ever live without you."
I said, "Is that you or the wine talking?"
She said, "It's me talking to the wine."

124

The first thing on my bucket list is to fill the bucket with wine.

125

A drunk got on a bus one day and sat down next to a priest.

The drunk stank of wine, his shirt was stained, his face was all red, and he had a half-empty bottle of wine sticking out of his pocket.

He opened his newspaper and started reading. A couple of minutes later, he asked the priest, "Father, what causes arthritis?"

The priest replied, "Mister, it's caused by loose living, being with cheap, wicked women, too much alcohol, and contempt for your fellow man."

"Imagine that," the drunk muttered. He returned to reading his paper.

The priest, thinking about what he had said, turned to the man and apologized. "I'm sorry, I didn't mean to come on so strong. How long have you had arthritis?"

"I don't have arthritis, Father," the drunk said, "but I just read in the paper that the Pope does."

126

I HAVE JOY IN MY HEART AND A GLASS OF WINE IN MY HAND. COINCIDENCE?

127

It doesn't matter if the glass is half empty or half full. There's clearly room for more wine.

128

A priest was driving down the road one day when he got stopped by a cop.

The cop smelled alcohol on the priest's breath and saw an empty wine bottle on the floor of the car.

He said to the priest, "Father, have you been drinking?"

The priest replied, "Only water, officer."

The cop then asked him, "Then why can I smell wine?"

The priest looked at the bottle and said, "Good Lord! He's done it again."

129

When you get a hangover from wine, it's called the grape depression.

130

I enjoy a glass of wine each night for its health benefits. The other glasses are for my witty comebacks and my flawless dance moves.

131

THE SECRET OF ENJOYING A GOOD BOTTLE OF WINE:

1. Open the bottle to allow it to breathe.
2. If it doesn't look like it's breathing, give it mouth-to-mouth.

132

IT'S FUNNY HOW **8** GLASSES OF WATER A DAY SEEMS IMPOSSIBLE...

But 8 glasses of wine can be done in one meal.

133

I read today that winemakers have developed a new
hybrid grape that acts as an anti-diuretic.
The aim is to reduce the number of trips to the bathroom that
older people have to make during the night.
They're going to call it, "Pinot More."
I heard it through the grapevine.

134

I recently went to my new doctor.

After two visits and exhaustive tests, he said I was doing "fairly well" for my age.

I was a bit worried about what he meant by that, so I asked him, "Do you think I'll live to be eighty, Doc?"

He looked at me and asked me, "Do you smoke or drink beer or wine?"

I said, "No, nothing like that. And I don't do drugs either."

He looked at me again and asked me, "Okay, do you eat rib-eye steaks and barbecued ribs?"

I said, "No, my old doctor told me that all red meat is very unhealthy."

He looked at me again and asked me, "Do you spend a lot of time in the sun, like playing golf, sailing, hiking, or bicycling?"

I replied, "No, nothing like that."

He looked at me again and asked me, "And do you gamble, drive fast cars, or have a lot of sex?"

I said, "No, nothing like that, Doc."

He looked at me again and said, "Then why do you even care?"

135

Did you know that wine doesn't make you fat?

It makes you lean . . .

against tables, chairs, floors, walls, and people.

136

I drank so much wine last night that when I walked across the dance floor to get another glass, I won the dance competition.

137

A woman was driving home in Northern Arizona, when she saw an elderly Navajo woman walking on the side of the road.

She stopped the car and asked the woman if she'd like a ride. The woman thanked her and got in the car.

After a few minutes, the Navajo woman noticed a brown bag on the back seat and asked the driver what was in the bag.

The driver said, "It's a bottle of wine. I got it for my husband."

The Navajo woman thought for a moment, then said, "Good trade."

138

People say that drinking milk makes you stronger.
Drink 5 glasses of milk and then try moving a wall.
Impossible?
Now drink 5 glasses of wine.
The wall moves by itself.

139

**EVERY BOX OF RAISINS IS A
TRAGIC TALE OF GRAPES THAT
COULD HAVE BEEN WINE.**

140

I can't wait for the day when I can drink wine with my kids instead of because of them.

141

At Christmastime, there's nothing I love more than sitting in front of a warm fire, mulled wine in hand, and singing Christmas songs until I slowly fall asleep.

Maybe that's why I'm no longer a fireman.

**Why don't they play
poker on the savanna?**

Too many cheetahs.

**What did the Buddhist say to the
hot dog vendor?**

Make me one with everything.

144

"I'm sorry for throwing red wine over all your dresses in the wardrobe last night," I told my girlfriend. "I've spent all day getting the stains out just to show how much you mean to me."
"Oh, that's really nice," she said. "What did you use to remove the stains?"
"Scissors," I replied.

145

WHAT DOES A VEGETARIAN ZOMBIE EAT?

"Graaaaaaaains!"

147

I wasn't going to visit my family this December, but my mom promised to make me Eggs Benedict.

So I'm going home for the hollandaise.

147

Why didn't the astronaut come home to his wife?

He needed his space.

148

I GOT FIRED FROM MY JOB AT THE BANK TODAY.

An old lady came in and asked me to check her balance, so I pushed her over.

149

Why are husbands like lawn mowers?

They're hard to get started, smell bad, and don't work half the time.

What did the blanket say as it fell off the bed?

"Oh, *sheet*!"

I like to spend every day as if it's my last.

Staying in bed and calling for a nurse to bring me more pudding.

152

WHY DO COW-MILKING STOOLS ONLY HAVE THREE LEGS?

'Cause the cow's got the udder!

153

How did Darth Vader know what Luke got him for Christmas?

He felt his presents.

154

What's the last thing that goes through a bug's mind when it hits a windshield?

Its butt.

155

What did the janitor say when he jumped out of the closet?

"Supplies!"

156

Imagine if Americans switched from pounds to kilograms overnight.

There would be mass confusion!

157

IT'S INAPPROPRIATE TO MAKE A "DAD JOKE" IF YOU ARE NOT A DAD.

It's a faux pa.

158

What did Batman say to Robin before they got in the car?

"Robin, get in the car."

160

A mother gets an invite to her friend's party and replies: Thanks for the invite! Just remember that I have small children, so you can expect us between the hours of crazy-late and never-showed-up.

159

I have an addiction to cheddar cheese.
But it's only mild.

161

MY HUSBAND AND I SHARE THE LOAD OF A NEWBORN BABY. I BREASTFEED BECAUSE HE CAN'T, AND HE SLEEPS BECAUSE I CAN'T.

162

Mom 1: Why is your son crying?
Mom 2: I asked him to put his shoes away.

163

What did our parents do to kill boredom before the internet?

I asked my 26 brothers and sisters and they didn't know either!

164

I OFTEN WALK A FINE LINE BETWEEN "SUPER-FUN MOM" AND "KINDA-PSYCHOTIC-MAYBE-WE-SHOULD-CALL-THE-AUTHORITIES MOM."

165

Why shouldn't you write with a broken pencil?

Because it's pointless!

166

Son: I'm learning to juggle, Mom!

Mom: Be careful. I was always told that when a group of clowns attack they always go for the juggler.

167

DAUGHTER: Mom, I'm getting my ombre done tomorrow, do you know how long it takes?

MOM: I don't know. . . . Your dad's the only hombre I've ever done.

168

Mom: Look at how this bimbo parked.
Daughter: Bimbo?
Mom: Yeah, the guy who lives across the street.
He's a bimbo.
Daughter: Mom, bimbo is a term for a stupid woman.
Mom: Oh . . . Well then, he's a bimbob.

169

Mom: What do you and your friends text about all day?
Daughter: I don't know, we don't really talk about
stuff, we just send each other memes all day.
Mom: Oh, is it a meme-ingful conversation?

170

What do you get when you put your wand in the Chamber of Secrets?

Hogwarts.

171

MOM, WHY DID THE CHICKEN CROSS THE ROAD?

I don't know, ask your dad!

A woman lives next to a graveyard with her family. A young husband and wife walk by on their way to see the neighboring house that's for sale and stop to talk with her.

Young wife: "Are there a lot of people moving into this neighborhood?"

Woman: "Oh yes. People are just dying to live next door to us!"

What kind of flowers are best for Mother's Day?

Mums.

174

WHY DID THEY HAVE TO RUSH THE MOMMY RATTLESNAKE TO THE DOCTOR ON MOTHER'S DAY?

She bit her tongue!

175

Why did the mommy cat want to go bowling on Mother's Day?

She was an alley cat.

176

What color flowers do mama cats like to get on Mother's Day?

Purrrrrrrple flowers.

177

What did the mommy pig put on her Mother's Day pancakes?

Hog cabin syrup.

178

What warm drink helps Mom relax on Mother's Day?

Calm-omile tea.

179

How do you get the kids to be quiet on Mother's Day morning?

Say, "Mum's the word."

180

How do you keep little cows quiet so their mommy can sleep late on Mother's Day?

Use the moooooote button.

181

WHY WAS THE HOUSE SO NEAT ON MOTHER'S DAY?

Because Mom spent all day Saturday cleaning it . . .

What did Eeyore say to his mom on Mother's Day when he served her breakfast in bed?

I hope thistle make you happy.

WHAT DID THE KITTENS GIVE THEIR MOM FOR MOTHER'S DAY?

A subscription to Good Mousekeeping.

184

One day Joe's mother turned to Joe's father and said, "It's such a nice day, I think I'll take Joe to the zoo."
"I wouldn't bother," said the father. "If they want him, let them come and get him!"

185

What has a long plume and wings and wears a red bow?

A Mother's Day pheasant.

186

WHAT KIND OF CANDY DO MOMS LOVE FOR MOTHER'S DAY?

Her-she's Kisses.

187

Why did the mommy horse want to race on a rainy Mother's Day?

She was a mudder.

188

Why did the bean children give their mom a sweater for Mother's Day?

She was chili . . .

189

What kind of flowers do yellow jacket mothers like for Mother's Day?

Bee-gonias.

190

Why did mom get a plate of English muffins on Mother's Day?

Her family wanted her to feel like a queen!

191

Why did the children put their joke book through the shredder?

It was Mother's Day and their dad told them to CUT the comedy.

192

What did the girl give her mom on Mother's Day to make her feel pampered?

A box of diapers (Pampers).

193

WHAT DID THE MOMMY CAT SAY WHEN HER KITTENS BROUGHT HER WARM MILK ON MOTHER'S DAY?

It's purrrrrfect.

194

WHO DO FLOWERS CELEBRATE ON MOTHER'S DAY?

Their chrysanthemums.

195

Why did the boy put the Mother's Day cupcakes in the freezer?

His sister told him to ice them.

196

Why did the dentist's children give their mommy so many gifts for Mother's Day?

They love toothee her smile.

197

Why was the cracker so happy to see his mom on Mother's Day?

Because he had been a wafer so long.

198

WHAT DID THE PANDA GIVE HIS MOMMY ON MOTHER'S DAY?

A bear hug.

199

How did the panda open her Mother's Day card?

With her bear hands.

200

What makes more noise than a child jumping on Mommy's bed on Mother's Day morning?

Two children jumping on Mommy's bed!

201

What kind of coffee was the alien mommy drinking on Mother's Day?

Starbucks.

202

Why did the boy make sweet potato pie for Mother's Day?

His mom always said his pie was yam-tastic.

203

Why was the grape late for Mother's Day brunch?

She got caught in a jam on the way.

204

WHY DID MOMMY'S GIFT ARRIVE THE DAY AFTER MOTHER'S DAY?

It was chocoLATE.

205

How did the alien boy write his Mother's Day poem?

In uni-verses.

206

What did the hermit crabs do on Mother's Day?

They shellabrated their mommy.

207

WHAT'S THE BEST THING A NEW MOM CAN GET FOR MOTHER'S DAY?

A long nap.

208

What dessert did the mommy cat get after her Mother's Day dinner?

Chocolate Mouse.

209

Why was the Mother's Day cake so hard?

It was a marble cake.

210

Why did the sea captain's mommy go out on Mother's Day?

To shop the sails.

211

What should you make Mom for dinner on Mother's Day?

Anything you want—she's just happy that she doesn't have to make it!

212

WHY WAS MOM SO HAPPY TO GO TO IHOP FOR PANCAKES ON MOTHER'S DAY?

She knew she wouldn't have to do any dishes.

213

What did the waiter say to the mommy dog when he served Mother's Day dinner?

Bone-appetit!

214

What was the mommy cat wearing to breakfast on Mother's Day?

She was still in her paw-jamas.

215

What did the banana's mommy get on Mother's Day?

Slippers.

216

WHY DO SONS LOVE MOTHER'S DAY SO MUCH?

Because it's always on son day (Sunday).

217

Why do moms hope it doesn't rain on Mother's Day?

So their kids can play outside!

218

Why was it so hard for the pirate to call his mom on Mother's Day?

Because she left the phone off the hook.

219

What did the Egyptian family do on Mother's Day?

Brought their mummy breakfast in bed.

220

WHAT DID THE LAZY BOY SAY TO HIS MOM ON MOTHER'S DAY WHEN SHE WAS ABOUT TO DO THE DISHES?

Relax mom . . . you can just do them in the morning.

221

What kind of sweets do astronaut moms like for Mother's Day?

Mars bars.

222

Who helped make Mother's Day breakfast for mama corn?

Pop-corn.

223

Why did the sisters give such a tiny gift to their mom for Mother's Day?

She was a minimum.

224

WHAT DO NICE PIRATES DO ON MOTHER'S DAY?

Take out the garrrrrrrrrrrbage without being asked.

225

Where did the reindeer family go for ice cream on Mother's Day?

Deery Queen.

226

What did the cheerleader bring her mom for breakfast on Mother's Day?

Cheerios.

227

What was Cleopatra's favorite day of the year?

Mummy's day.

228

WHY DIDN'T THE MAID'S CHILDREN WAKE HER UP?

It was Mother's Day and they let her sweep in.

229

When does Mother's Day come before St. Patrick's Day?

In the dictionary!

230

WHY COULDN'T MOM PUT HER CROCHET PROJECT DOWN ON MOTHER'S DAY?

She was hooked on it.

231

Why were the rope children so quiet on Mother's Day?

They were trying not to be knotty.

232

What can reindeer mommies see on Mother's Day that no other moms can see?

Their reindeer children.

233

Which is the most special Sunday in Egypt?

Mummy's Day.

234

WHERE DID THE COW FAMILY GO ON MOTHER'S DAY?

The moo-vies.

235

Which restaurant did the buccaneer take his mom to for Mother's Day?

Long John Silver's.

Whom do panda children celebrate on Mother's Day?

Child-BEARers.

What did the Martians wear to Mother's Day dinner?

Space suits.

238

Which day does Cherry Garcia's mommy like the most?

Mother's Day Sundae.

239

What's the easiest way to wake Mom up on Mother's Day?

Put a cat on the bed . . . while the dog's there!

240

What if mom still doesn't wake up with a cat and dog on the bed?

Throw a mouse on the bed!

241

WHAT SHOULD YOU NEVER GIVE A MOMMY DENTIST ON MOTHER'S DAY?

A plaque!

242

WHY DID THE KIDS GIVE THEIR MOM A BLANKET FOR MOTHER'S DAY?

Because they thought she was the coolest mom.

243

What happens at the needle's house on Mother's Day at 8pm?

Thread-time (bed time).

244

What did the puppies make their mom for Mother's Day breakfast?

Pooched eggs.

245

Where did the spider learn how to make a Mother's Day gift?

On the web.

246

What did Chewbacca bake for his mom on Mother's Day?

Chocolate Chip Wookiees.

247

What magazine did the mommy cow read while her calves made a Mother's Day brunch?

Cows-mopolitan.

248

HOW DID THE MOMMY CAT FEEL ON MOTHER'S DAY?

She was in a great mewd.

249

Why didn't the teddy bear's mommy want a big meal on Mother's Day?

She was already stuffed!

**How do piglets wake their mama up on
Mother's Day?**

With hogs and kisses.

**Why couldn't the digital clock make dinner for
Mother's Day?**

He had no hands.

252

When would you hit a Mother's Day cake with a hammer?

When it's a pound cake.

253

DEFINITION: *BETRAYAL* (NOUN)—THE FIRST TIME A CHILD LEARNS THEIR MOM'S NAME ISN'T ACTUALLY "MOM."

254

IF AT FIRST YOU DON'T SUCCEED, TRY DOING IT THE WAY YOUR MOM TOLD YOU TO IN THE BEGINNING.

255

Why did the scarecrow win an award?

He was outstanding in his field.

256

I was sitting in traffic the other day.

That's probably why I got run over.

257

Sometimes I tuck my knees into my chest and lean forward.

That's just how I roll.

258

What's red and shaped like a bucket?

A blue bucket painted red.

259

WHY DON'T ANTS GET SICK?

They have anty-bodies.

260

What do you call a fish with no eye?

Fssshh.

261

Why do you smear peanut butter on the road?

To go with the traffic jam.

262

When is your door not actually a door?

When it's actually ajar.

263

MY GRANDFATHER HAS THE HEART OF A LION. . . .

. . . And a lifetime ban from the New York City Zoo.

264

What's green, fuzzy, and would hurt if it fell on you out of a tree?

A pool table.

265

What's green and has wheels?

Grass. I lied about the wheels.

266

A COMMUNIST JOKE ISN'T FUNNY . . .

. . . unless everyone gets it.

267

My new girlfriend told me I'm terrible in bed.

I don't think it's fair to make a judgement like that in less than a minute.

268

What happens to pastors who eat chili dogs?

They have to sit in their own pew.

269

Why can't you hear a pterodactyl go to the bathroom?

Because the pee is silent.

270

Cosmetic surgery used to be such a taboo subject.

Now you can talk about Botox and nobody raises an eyebrow.

271

What do you call someone who immigrated to Sweden?

Artificial Swedener.

272

HAVE YOU HEARD ABOUT THE CORDUROY PILLOW?

It's making headlines.

273

What do you call a man with no arms and no legs in a pool?

Bob.

What do you call a man who can't stand?

Neil.

What's the dumbest animal in the jungle?

A polar bear.

276

I'M THINKING ABOUT REMOVING MY SPINE.

I feel like it's only holding me back.

277

Did you hear about the two thieves who stole a calendar?

They each got six months.

278

I'M TERRIFIED OF ELEVATORS . . .

. . . so I'm going to start taking steps to avoid them.

279

Have you heard of the band 923 Megabytes?

Probably not, they haven't had a gig yet.

280

What do you call a psychic little person who has escaped from prison?

A small medium at large.

281

I used to hate facial hair . . .

. . . but then it grew on me.

How many tickles does it take to make an octopus laugh?

Ten tickles.

283

I used to be addicted to the hokey pokey . . .

. . . but then I turned myself around.

284

WHAT'S THE MOST TERRIFYING WORD IN NUCLEAR PHYSICS?

"Oops!"

285

I watched hockey before it was cool.

They were basically swimming.

286

THERE'S NO HOLE IN YOUR SHOE?

Then how'd you get your foot in it?

287

A cowherd counted 48 cows on his property.

But when he rounded them up, he had 50.

288

**When the two radio antennae got married,
it was a nice ceremony.**

But the reception was amazing.

Why couldn't the bicycle stand up?

Because it was too tired (two-tired).

A chicken coop only has two doors.

If it had four, it would be a chicken sedan.

291

THREE FISH ARE IN A TANK.

One asks the others, "How do you drive this thing?"

292

Why don't crabs donate?

Because they're shellfish.

293

What did the parrot say when he turned eighty?

"Aye, matey."

294

HOW DOES YOUR FELINE SHOP?

By reading a catalogue.

295

It's hard to teach kleptomaniacs humor.

They take things so literally.

296

Sunny-side up, scrambled, or an omelet?

It doesn't matter. They're all eggcellent.

297

Don't worry if you miss a gym session.

Everything will work out.

298

Ever tried to eat a clock?

It's time-consuming.

299

Who can jump higher than a house?

Pretty much anyone. (Houses can't jump.)

300

WHAT DO AN APPLE AND AN ORANGE HAVE IN COMMON?

Neither one can drive.

301

Why did the businessman invest in Smith & Wollensky?

He wanted to steak his claim.

302

FIVE GUYS WALK INTO A BAR.

You think one of them would've seen it.

303

**What did the mother bullet
say to the daddy bullet?**

We're going to have a BB!

304

**This sweet ride has four wheels
and flies. It's . . .**

A garbage truck.

305

How many bugs do you need to rent out an apartment?

Tenants.

306

I want to go camping every year.

That trip was in tents.

307

WAIT, YOU DON'T WANT TO HEAR A JOKE ABOUT POTASSIUM?

K.

308

How do you organize a space-themed hurrah?

You planet.

Knock, knock

Who's there?

Sadie.

Sadie who?

Sadie magic word and watch me disappear!

Knock, knock.

Who's there?

Ivor.

Ivor who?

Ivor you let me in or I`ll climb through the window.

311

KNOCK, KNOCK.
Who's there?
ABBY.
Abby who?
ABBY BIRTHDAY TO YOU!

312

Boy 1: I think my mom's getting serious about straightening up my room once and for all.

Boy 2: How do you know?

Boy 1: She's learning to drive a bulldozer.

313

KNOCK, KNOCK.
Who's there?
BROCCOLI!
Broccoli who?
**BROCCOLI DOESN'T HAVE
A LAST NAME, SILLY.**

314

Knock, knock.
Who's there?
Scold.
Scold who?
Scold enough out here to go ice skating.

315

Knock, knock.
Who's there?
Justin.
Justin who?
**Just in the neighborhood,
thought I would drop by.**

316

Knock, knock.
Who's there?
Two knee.
Two knee who?
Two-knee fish!

317

Knock, knock.
Who's there?
Hop.
Hop who?
Hoppy Mother's Day!

318

Knock, knock.
Who's there?
Isabell.
Isabell who?
Is a bell working?

319

Knock, knock
Who's there?
Alex.
Alex who?
Alex-plain later!

320

KNOCK! KNOCK!
Who's there?
ANNIE.
Annie who?
ANNIE BODY HOME?

321

Knock, knock!
Who's there?
Cook.
Cook who?
Hey! Who are you calling cuckoo?

322

KNOCK! KNOCK!
Who's there?
DISHES.
Dishes who?
DISH IS A NICE PLACE!

Knock, knock.
Who's there?
Althea.
Althea who?
Althea later alligator!

Knock, knock.
Who's there?
CD.
CD who?
CD guy on your doorstep?

325

Knock, knock.

Who's there?

Iowa.

Iowa who?

Iowa big apology to the owner of that red car!

326

Knock, knock.

Who's there?

Viper.

Viper who?

Viper nose, it's running!

327

Knock, knock.
Who's there?
Abbot.
Abbot who?
Abbot you don't know who this is!

328

KNOCK! KNOCK!
Who's there?
EGG.
Egg who?
EGGSTREMELY DISAPPOINTED YOU STILL DON'T RECOGNIZE ME.

Knock knock.
Who's there?
Four eggs.
Four eggs who?
Four eggsellent reasons, I wish that my identity remain concealed.

KNOCK! KNOCK!
Who's there?
MOM AND DAD.
Mom and Dad who?
EXACTLY SON, YOU ARE ADOPTED.

331

Knock knock.
Who's there?
I am.
I am who?
Ooh, quite the existentialist I see.

332

Knock knock!
Who's there?
Cereal.
Cereal who?
Cereal pleasure to meet you!

KNOCK! KNOCK!
Who's there?
HO-HO.
Ho-ho who?
**YOU KNOW, YOUR SANTA IMPRESSION
COULD USE A LITTLE WORK.**

334

Knock knock!
Who's there?
Aardvark.
Aardvark who?
Aardvark a hundred miles for one of your smiles!

335

Knock knock!
Who's there?
Yule log.
Yule log who?
Yule log the door after you let me in, won't you?

336

Knock knock.

Who's there?

Stopwatch.

Stopwatch who?

Stopwatcha doin' and open the stupid door.

337

Knock knock.

Who's there?

Wire.

Wire who?

**Wire we here? Why is anybody here?
Let's just have a drink.**

338

WHAT'S THE DIFFERENCE BETWEEN A NEW HUSBAND AND A NEW DOG?

A new dog only takes a few months to train.

339

Woman one: My husband's cooking is so bad!

Woman two: How bad is it?

Woman one: Well, the kids have started praying after the meal.

340

Woman one: I got so mad at my GPS today that I told it to go to hell!
Woman two: Did that work?
Woman one: Well, it took me to my in-laws' house.

341

Is the glass half empty or half full?

Who cares, either way there's room for more wine in it.

178

342

ALWAYS GIVE 100% AT WORK . . .

12% on Monday
23% on Tuesday
40% on Wednesday
20% on Thursday
5% on Fridays

And remember . . .
When you're having a really bad day and it seems like people are trying to piss you off, remember it takes 42 muscles to frown and only 4 to extend your finger and flip them off.

343

WHY DID THE MONSTER'S MOTHER KNIT HIM THREE SOCKS?

She heard he grew another foot!

344

A female patient's family gathered to hear what the specialists had to say.

"Things don't look good. The only chance is a brain transplant. This is an experimental procedure. It might work, but the bad news is that brains are very expensive, and you will have to pay the costs yourselves."

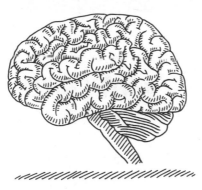

"Well, how much does a brain cost?" asked the relatives.

"For a male brain, $500,000. For a female brain, $200,000."

Some of the younger male relatives tried to look shocked, but all the men nodded because they thought they understood. A few actually smirked. But the patient's daughter was unsatisfied and asked, "Why the difference in price between male brains and female brains?"

"A standard pricing practice," said the head of the team. "Women's brains have to be marked down because they have actually been used."

ALSO AVAILABLE

"An all-purpose guide to ensuring that no one finds you as amusing as you do."
—*Cool Dad Mag*

Dad Jokes

More than **400** Unbearable, Groan-inducing One-liners Sure to Make You the Most Deadliest Dad with a Pun

Joe Kerz

COMING SOON!

REALLY BAD

Dad Jokes

More than **400** Unbearable, Groan-inducing Wisecracks Sure to Make You the Funniest Father With a Quip

— Joe Kerz —

EXTREMELY INAPPROPRIATE

Dad Jokes

Hazardous Jokes, Side-Splitting Puns, and Hilarious One-Liners to Make You the **Master of Questionable Comedy**

JOE KERZ